Animal Neighbours
Mouse

Stephen Savage

HODDER
Wayland

An imprint of Hodder Children's Books

Animal Neighbours

Titles in this series:

Badger • Bat • Deer • Fox • Hare • Hedgehog
Mole • Mouse • Otter • Owl • Rat • Swallow

Conceived and produced for Hodder Wayland by

Nutshell
MEDIA

Intergen House, 65–67 Western Road, Hove BN3 2JQ, UK
www.nutshellmedialtd.co.uk

Commissioning Editor: Vicky Brooker
Designer: Tim Mayer
Illustrator: Jackie Harland
Picture Research: Glass Onion Pictures

Published in Great Britain in 2003 by Hodder Wayland, an imprint of Hodder Children's Books.

British Library Cataloguing in Publication Data
Savage, Stephen, 1965-
Mouse. – (Animal neighbours)
1. Mice – Juvenile literature
I. Title
599.3'53

ISBN 0 7502 4474 7

Printed and bound in Hong Kong.

Hodder Children's Books
A division of Hodder Headline Limited
338 Euston Road, London NW1 3BH

Cover photograph: A mouse stands up on its hind feet to sniff the air for food.
Title page: A mouse looks out from a loaf of bread.

Picture acknowledgements
FLPA 7 (Martin Withers), 9, 10, 13, 20 (Jurgen & Christine Sohns), 24 (By Silvestris), 28 right, 28 bottom
(Jurgen & Christine Sohns); naturepl.com 27 (Georgette Douwma); NHPA *Title page*, 19, 21 (Stephen
Dalton), 22 (Joe Blossom), 23 (Ant Photo Library), 25 (Manfred Danegger), 28 left (Joe Blossom);
Oxford Scientific Films *Cover* (Rodger Jackman), 6 (Michael Fogden), 8 (Tony Bomford), 11 (Zig
Leszczynski/AA), 12 (Kathie Atkinson), 14 (OSF), 15, 16 (Rodger Jackman), 17 (Satoshi Kuribayashi),
26 (Rodger Jackman), 28 top (Tony Bomford).

Contents

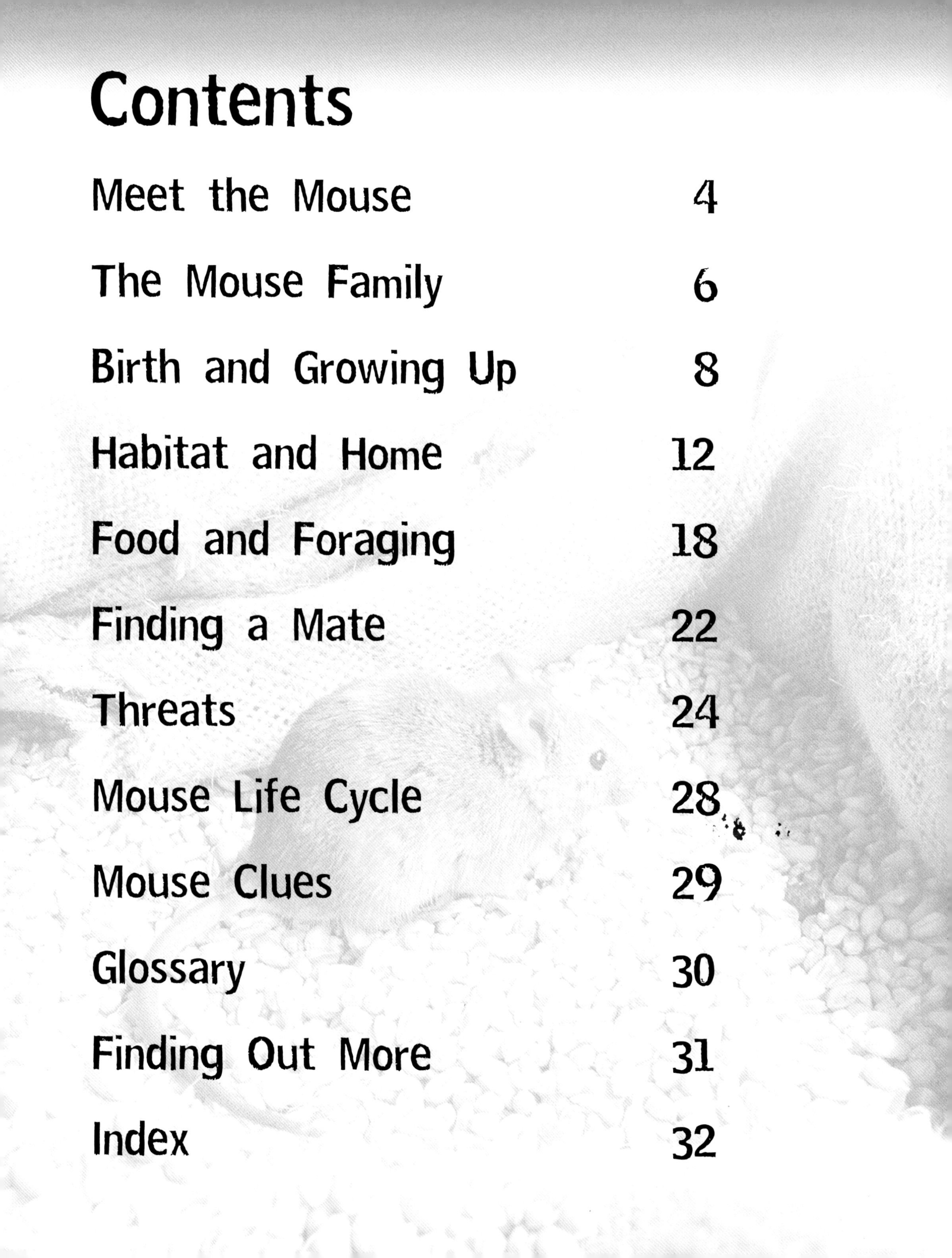

Meet the Mouse 4

The Mouse Family 6

Birth and Growing Up 8

Habitat and Home 12

Food and Foraging 18

Finding a Mate 22

Threats 24

Mouse Life Cycle 28

Mouse Clues 29

Glossary 30

Finding Out More 31

Index 32

Meet the Mouse

Mice are small, agile rodents. They have adapted to almost every habitat, from fields and forests, to deserts, towns and cities. Mice live everywhere in the world apart from the polar regions.

This book looks at the house mouse and why it is the most widespread of all the mouse species.

▲ **This shows the size of a house mouse compared to an adult human hand.**

A house mouse. ▶

Fur

Mice have oily fur that is warm and protective.

Body

The mouse's body has tiny bones, which means it can squeeze through holes as small as 1 cm. If the mouse's head fits through a hole, the body can squeeze through, too.

Tail

The mouse's thin tail is almost hairless. It helps the mouse balance, especially when standing on its hind legs.

Feet

Mice have small, clawed feet, which are ideal for running and climbing.

MOUSE FACTS

The house mouse's scientific name is *Mus musculus*, from the Latin word *musculus* meaning 'little mouse'.

The word 'mouse' comes from the word for 'thief' in Sanskrit, an ancient Indian language.

Male mice are known as bucks, females as does and young mice as pups.

The house mouse's body is about 9 cm long without the tail. The tail is almost as long as the body. Adult house mice weigh about 30 g.

Ears

Mice have large ears and an excellent sense of hearing, which is their main sense for detecting danger.

Eyes

Mice have poor eyesight and they cannot see things in colour. Since they move around mostly in the dark, mice rely more on their whiskers to find their way around.

Nose

The mouse has a good sense of smell for finding food. It also uses smell to recognise other mice from their scent-marks.

Teeth

Like all rodents, mice have chisel-shaped teeth to gnaw food, which continue to grow throughout their lives. The teeth must be ground down by gnawing on hard objects to stop them growing too long.

Whiskers

Whiskers grow from sensitive pits on the mouse's face. They help the mouse to find its way through tunnels, or around its territory in the dark.

The Mouse Family

Mice belong to the largest group of mammals, the rats and mice family. Scientists call this group the 'mouse-like group of rodents'. It includes various species of mice, rats, voles, gerbils, hamsters and lemmings.

All mouse-like rodents are mouse-shaped, but they vary greatly in body size, and the size and shape of their ears, tail and feet. Many dig burrow systems where they live in colonies.

▼ **This southern grasshopper mouse is eating a freshly killed harvest mouse.**

BREEDING

People have been breeding mice for over 4,000 years. In ancient Egypt, Greece and China they were kept for luck in temples or homes, or used to predict the future. Selective breeding has created over 7,500 colour varieties which are kept as pets. These include white, piebald (two-coloured), chocolate-tan, blue, champagne and silver. Mice are also bred for pet snake food, and bred in laboratories for medical studies.

Most mice are omnivores that feed on seeds, insects and carrion, but a few species are carnivores. The grasshopper mouse lives in the grasslands of the USA. Apart from grasshoppers, it also eats scorpions and even other mice, some of which are bigger than itself.

The tiny harvest mouse has a clever way of hiding from predators. It builds nests attached to the stalks of grasses and crops, 30–100 centimetres above the ground, where it retreats in times of danger. The dusky hopping mouse from Australia escapes danger by bounding along on its hind legs like a kangaroo.

◀ A harvest mouse peers out from its nest, which is perched up above the ground.

7

Birth and Growing Up

In the countryside, most house mice are born between March and October, when there is the most food available. House mice living in towns and cities can be born at almost any time of the year.

Before she gives birth, a pregnant doe will prepare a nest in a warm, dark place. This could be under a garage roof, in a storage box in an attic, or in the corner of a barn. If it is her first litter, the doe will have to build the nest from scratch. But she may already have a nest from previous litters.

A litter of new-born ▶ pups huddle together to keep warm while their mother forages for food.

MOUSE PUPS

New-born pups are about 30 mm long and weigh about 2.5 mg.

The average sized litter is five or six pups, although a doe can give birth to as many as thirteen.

The young pups are born pink, blind and completely helpless. They are hairless except for the tiny whiskers on their faces, and their eyes and ears are tightly closed. The new-born pups have to rely on their mother for food and protection. She cleans and suckles them several times a day, only leaving the nest to find food. When she returns to the nest the pups recognise their mother by her smell.

Mouse pups grow rapidly. By the time they are 10 days old they are covered in fur. Their eyes and ears open when they are 14 days old.

▼ A doe suckles her fully furred pups.

Early days

Between 2–3 weeks old, the young mice begin to make short trips from their nest and explore their surroundings. The pups start to learn the skills they will need to survive on their own, such as finding their own food, learning to be secretive and avoiding danger.

By 3–4 weeks old, the young mice are fully weaned and leave the nest for good. By now, their mother is pregnant again.

GROOMING

Keeping clean is a regular activity for mice, and a skill that young mice will need to learn. Mice groom their fur with their teeth and scratch themselves with their hind feet. They use their front paws to 'wash' their face and their teeth for nibbling fur. Mice also groom each other with their teeth to show friendship.

▼ Two young house mice nibble at a tasty blackberry.

As it leaves the nest where it was born, the young mouse faces many dangers and most do not survive their first year. Apart from the threat of predators such as cats, foxes and birds of prey, young mice are driven away by adult mice, who are often aggressive towards the young. The greater the number of mice living in a place, the further the young mouse will have to travel from where it was born.

◄ Many young house mice are eaten by predators, such as this long-eared owl.

Habitat and Home

In towns and cities there are lots of places for mice to live. They make their homes in holes and cracks in walls, buildings and bridges. Mice often live in houses, either in the space between the walls, under floorboards, or in attics. In sheds or garages they live amongst cardboard boxes and flowerpots. While some mice live permanently in houses, others only enter homes in the winter, when they are looking for food and warmth.

▼ Storage jars make useful stepping stones for this mouse exploring a kitchen.

Elsewhere in towns and cities, parks, warehouses and railway stations provide shelter and food for house mice. In zoos and wildlife parks, house mice live in enclosures alongside rhinoceroses, monkeys and other animals.

HISTORY

The house mouse originally came from Asia. About 4,000 years ago it spread to Europe, and now lives in almost every part of the world. At first the mouse followed the spread of farming, living off crops such as wheat. Then it followed people as they traded with other countries. Mice that stowed away on ships were able to travel across seas and oceans.

In the countryside, house mice often live in farm buildings such as barns. They are especially common on farms where crops are grown and grain is stored. Some mice live in nearby fields, hedgerows or derelict buildings.

▼ This house mouse lives in a field of corn, which provides its favourite food.

▲ A doe gathers scraps of material to make a nest.

The nest

Mice build their nests in places that are dark and warm, safe from the prying eyes of predators. The doe shreds a variety of available materials with her teeth and weaves them together with the help of her front feet to make the nest. Mouse nests are roughly ball-shaped and about 10 centimetres in diameter.

Urban mice use paper, sacks, clothing, roof insulation, string, or other soft materials to make their nests. Favourite nest sites include storage boxes, drawers, underneath kitchen appliances, or within the upholstery of furniture.

In the countryside, the nest is made from more natural materials such as dried grass, leaves or straw. Nests are made in farm buildings, bales of straw or even underneath hedgerows. Occasionally, house mice build a tunnel system or make a nest in another animal's disused burrow.

COLD HOME

The most unusual nest site for house mice is in a cold store, living at temperatures of −10 °C. In almost total darkness, both males and females tunnel and feed on the frozen meat. A nest is made for rearing young using the meat's hessian wrapping. Mice living in these cold conditions become larger and heavier. Their fat helps to keep them warm.

Once it is built, each mouse nest will probably be used to raise several litters of pups. Does sometimes nest together and help to nurse each other's pups. This is most likely with does that are related.

▼ This house mouse has made its nest in some old stuffing in a workshop.

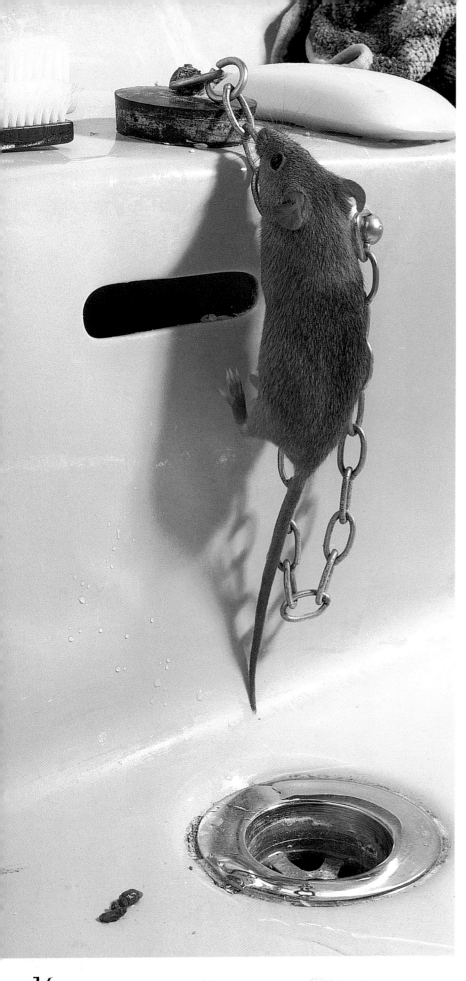

Territory

House mice live in small groups containing several does and one dominant male. Each group lives within a home range, or territory, which is usually no more than 9 metres in diameter.

The mice in each group scent-mark the borders of their territory with urine, so that other mice know the territory belongs to them. The dominant male then defends it from intruders. Rural mice are more defensive of their territory than those living in towns and cities.

Mice memorise the pathways in their territory and use the same routes every night. They find their way in the dark by touch using the long whiskers on their nose.

◀ **Mice are excellent climbers. This one is using a plug chain to climb out of a slippery sink.**

House mice are nocturnal animals, which means they are mostly active at night. However, they can usually be heard scuttling around behind a wall during the day. A mouse can leap up to 30 centimetres from the ground and climb up a brick wall. It can run along the tops of pipes and electrical cables and drop 2.5 metres to the floor.

◀ A house mouse leaps using its powerful back legs while the tail is used for balance.

COMMUNICATION

Mice can often be heard making squeaking sounds, but they make many calls that we do not hear because they are too quiet for our level of hearing. These quieter calls are social messages to nearby mice, or for calling a lost pup. The calls only travel short distances, which prevents predators from hearing them.

Food and Foraging

Mice are omnivores. They eat parts of plants, seeds, fruit, insects and carrion. Occasionally they eat worms, woodlice and fungi. Rural house mice feed on cereal crops or cereal grain in grain stores.

▼ House mice are at the centre of several food chains. (The illustrations are not to scale.)

Mouse food chain

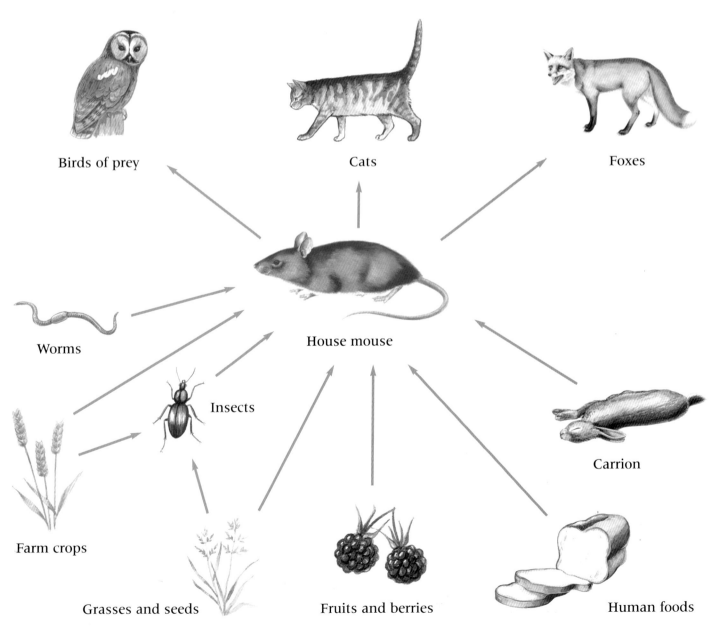

Birds of prey

Cats

Foxes

Worms

House mouse

Insects

Carrion

Farm crops

Grasses and seeds

Fruits and berries

Human foods

The house mouse's favourite food is grain, or food containing grain such as bread and biscuits. Mice will eat almost any human food, although unlike the cartoon mice we see on television, cheese is not one of their favourites. Urban mice often eat foods high in protein or fat, such as bacon and butter, or high in sugar, such as chocolate and sweets. These foods provide lots of energy and fat for warmth.

◀ **This house mouse has eaten its way into a loaf of bread.**

Foraging

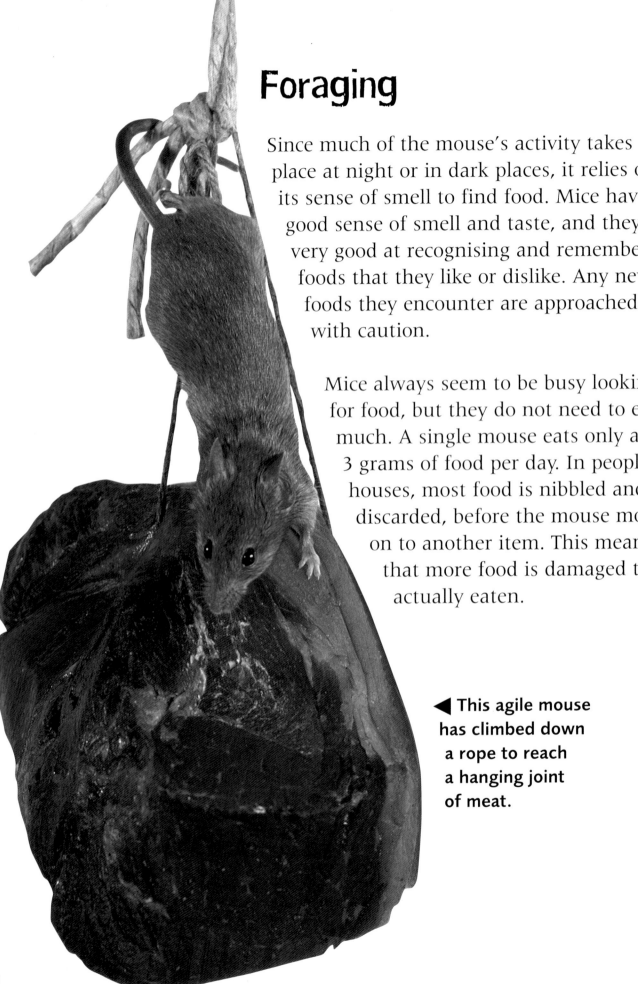

Since much of the mouse's activity takes place at night or in dark places, it relies on its sense of smell to find food. Mice have a good sense of smell and taste, and they are very good at recognising and remembering foods that they like or dislike. Any new foods they encounter are approached with caution.

Mice always seem to be busy looking for food, but they do not need to eat much. A single mouse eats only about 3 grams of food per day. In people's houses, most food is nibbled and discarded, before the mouse moves on to another item. This means that more food is damaged than actually eaten.

◀ **This agile mouse has climbed down a rope to reach a hanging joint of meat.**

▲ When mice gnaw through electric cables like this one it can be dangerous for both the mouse and the household.

Water

House mice drink water regularly if it is available, but they are able to survive without drinking because they use the small amounts of water that are present in their food. This is probably an ability inherited from their Asian ancestors, who had fewer towns and cities to get water, food and shelter. If mice do not get enough water, however, it reduces their ability to breed.

UNUSUAL FOODS

Apart from human food, house mice also eat some very strange items, such as plaster, glue, soap, candles and wood. They probably eat these items simply because they are something to nibble and they are attracted to them by their smell. Mice can do a lot of damage chewing through electrical wiring, damaging furniture or stored items such as books and documents.

21

Finding a Mate

When they are 5 weeks old, does are ready to mate. Bucks usually have to wait until they are 10 weeks old because they have to set up their own territory first. This is because does will only mate with the dominant male of the group. After mating, the buck leaves the doe and plays no part in rearing the young.

▼ A group of mice may start with just a male and female.

The pups are born about 20 days after mating. This, together with the young age that mice start mating, is why house mice breed so successfully. A doe gives birth every three to four weeks and can have up to ten litters a year.

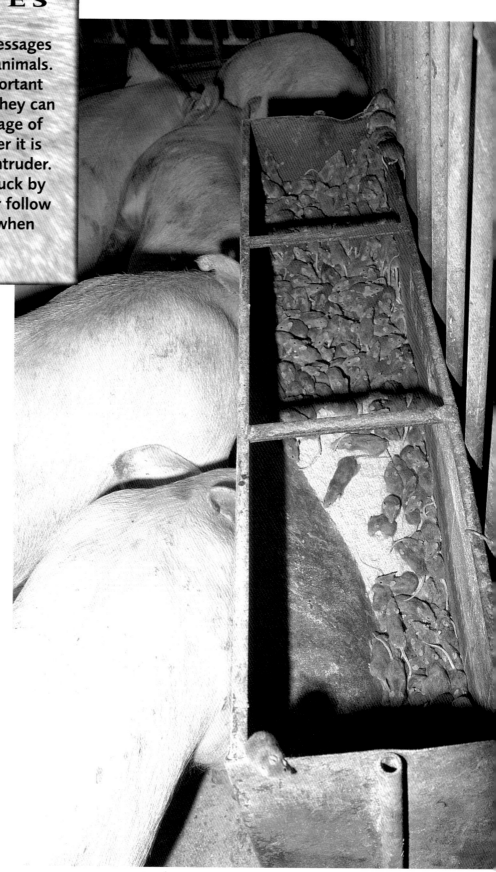

PHEROMONES

Pheromones are chemical messages sent out from the bodies of animals. These messages are an important part of a mouse's daily life. They can be used to tell the sex and age of another mouse, and whether it is from the same group or an intruder. A buck can avoid another buck by detecting its pheromones, or follow the pheromones of a doe when looking for a mate.

▶ A plague of hundreds of mice in a commercial piggery in Australia.

Sometimes the number of mice in an area can become very high, which causes an increase in fighting and squabbles between bucks. Overcrowding can cause some of the females in a group to temporarily or even permanently stop producing young. This helps to prevent the mice numbers increasing faster than the amount of space and food available.

Threats

Mice face threats from many predators. In the countryside, they are important prey for a wide range of animals. Owls, kestrels and other birds of prey swoop down on them in fields. Foxes and badgers hunt mice in woodlands, digging up their nests or catching the young as they first leave the nest. Two similar predators, the weasel and the larger stoat, both prey on house mice. The mouse's only defences are caution, moving around under cover, and speed when detected.

▼ A kestrel swoops down on a house mouse just outside the entrance to its nest.

A major predator of mice is the domestic cat. Many people think of cats as the mouse's worst enemy. While some cats are very good at catching mice, others would rather just curl up in front of the fire. Some cats, such as farm cats, are not kept as pets but for their ability to catch mice.

▼ Domestic cats often kill mice because they have a strong hunting instinct.

DOMESTIC CATS

Early civilisations domesticated wild cats to catch mice. The Phoenicians, who lived on the Mediterranean coast about 3,000 years ago, are thought to have brought the first domesticated cats to Europe on cargo ships in about 900 BC. They were probably kept on the ships to catch mice. The Romans introduced cats to Britain by about AD 300, when they occupied part of Britain.

People and mice

The mouse's worst enemy is people. Sometimes house mice live behind a wall and hardly ever enter the main parts of a house. But most mice will forage in kitchens and other parts of the house, taking advantage of the way we store food and rubbish.

Mice not only eat our foods, they contaminate it by nibbling or leaving droppings, making it unfit to eat. They can also carry diseases, especially in their urine. On farms, mice can damage food kept for livestock. For these reasons, people have waged war on the house mouse for almost as long as mice have lived with people.

▲ Mice have been a pest ever since people started growing crops, especially after harvesting, when grain is stored.

A variety of traps and poisons are used to kill mice. Poisoned grain is left in places for mice to find, but this only works if the mice eat enough of it. House mice have a good memory for tastes and will avoid any foods that taste bad. Also, many mice have become immune to poisons, so they are not always a successful killer. Some people believe that mice should be caught using harmless traps and released away from houses rather than killing them.

▼ Some house mice have learned to eat the cheese without setting off the mouse trap.

Mouse Life Cycle

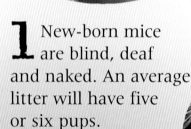

1 New-born mice are blind, deaf and naked. An average litter will have five or six pups.

2 Ten days after birth the pups are covered in fur. Their eyes and ears open when they are 14 days old.

5 A doe can produce her first litter at the age of 5 weeks. Bucks have to wait until they can secure a territory, usually after the age of 10 weeks.

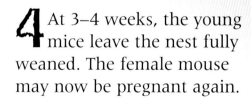

4 At 3–4 weeks, the young mice leave the nest fully weaned. The female mouse may now be pregnant again.

3 At about 18 days old the young mice leave the nest for the first time and start to forage for food.

Mouse Clues

Look out for the following clues to help you find signs of a mouse:

Nest
Shredded paper or other materials may be a sign that mice are nesting nearby. The nest itself will usually be out of sight, but one may be found in an airing cupboard, or boxes in a loft or garage.

Gnawing
Look for signs of gnawing on wooden objects such as boxes and furniture, especially where things are stored out of the way. Teeth marks are small and usually appear lighter than the rest of the wood. Sawdust may also be visible.

Droppings
Mouse droppings are found along trails frequently used by mice. They are small, black and rod-shaped, with pointed ends.

3–6 mm

Urine
Urine is deposited as scent trails. Sometimes urine pillars form in special places within a mouse's territory. These are a mixture of urine, grease, dirt and sometimes droppings.

Sounds
Mice can be quite noisy. You may hear gnawing, scratching or even scampering behind a wall. Mice also make a squeaking call.

Smell
Mice have a musky smell, particularly the males. Places where mice urinate frequently may also smell, as do the urine pillars.

Footprints
Mice have five toes on their back feet but only four toes on their front feet. A small drag mark where the tail touches the ground may also be visible behind the footprints.

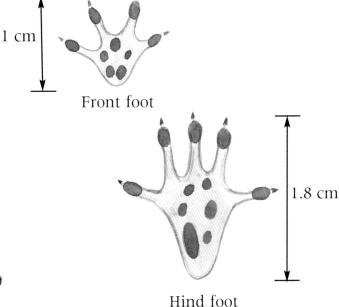

1 cm

Front foot

1.8 cm

Hind foot

Glossary

buck A male mouse. Male deer, rabbits and squirrels are also called bucks.

carnivores Animals that eat mainly other animals.

carrion The body of a dead animal that is found and eaten by another animal.

cereal crops Crops such as wheat, barley and maize, which produce grain that is used for food.

colonies Groups of the same type of animal that live together.

doe A female mouse. Female deer, rabbits and squirrels are also called does.

domestic Animals that have been tamed to be kept as a pet or as a working animal.

dominant The largest, strongest animal of the group.

forage To search for food.

habitat The area where an animal or plant naturally lives.

litter A group of young animals born at the same time from the same mother.

omnivores Animals that eat both plants and other animals.

predator An animal that eats other animals.

prey Animals that are killed and eaten by predators.

pup A young mouse. Young dogs, seals and bats are also called pups.

rodents A group of mammals that have two long, front teeth in each jaw for gnawing food. Mice, rats, squirrels, porcupines and beavers are all rodents.

selective breeding The breeding of different animals together to create a specific characteristic, such as colour.

suckle When a mother allows her young to drink milk from her teats.

territory The area that is defended and controlled by an animal.

urban A habitat in a town or city.

weaned A young mammal is weaned when it stops taking milk from its mother and eats only solid food.

Finding Out More

Other books to read

Animal Young: Mammals by Rod Theodorou (Heinemann, 1999)

Classification: Animal Kingdom by Kate Whyman (Hodder Wayland, 2000)

Classifying Living Things: Classifying Mammals by Andrew Solway (Heinemann, 2003)

From Egg to Adult: The Life Cycle of Mammals by Mike Unwin (Heinemann, 2003)

Illustrated Encyclopedia of Animals by Fran Pickering (Chrysalis, 2003)

Junior Nature Guides: Mammals (Chrysalis, 2003)

Life Cycles: Cats and Other Mammals by Sally Morgan (Chrysalis, 2001)

Living Nature: Mammals by Angela Royston (Chrysalis, 2002)

My Pet: Rats and Mice by Honor Head (Chrysalis, 2001)

New Encyclopedia of Mammals by David Macdonald (OUP, 2001)

Reading About Mammals by Anna Claybourne (Watts, 1999)

The Wayland Book of Common British Mammals by Shirley Thompson (Hodder Wayland, 2000)

Weird Wildlife: Mammals by Jen Green (Chrysalis, 2002)

What's the Difference?: Mammals by Stephen Savage (Hodder Wayland, 2002)

Wild Britain: Towns & Cities by R. & L. Spilsbury (Heinemann, 2003)

Organisations to contact

Countryside Foundation for Education
PO Box 8, Hebden Bridge HX7 5YJ
www.countrysidefoundation.org.uk
An organisation that produces training and teaching materials to help the understanding of the countryside and its problems.

English Nature
Northminster House, Peterborough, Cambridgeshire PE1 1UA
www.englishnature.org.uk
A government body that promotes the conservation of English wildlife and the natural environment.

The Mammal Society
2B Inworth Street, London SW11 3EP
www.abdn.ac.uk/mammal/newsite/
This organisation promotes the study and conservation of British mammals.

Wildlife Watch
National Office, The Kiln, Waterside, Mather Road, Newark NG24 1WT
www.wildlifetrusts.org
The junior branch of the Wildlife Trusts, a network of local Wildlife Trusts caring for nearly 2,500 nature reserves, from rugged coastline to urban wildlife havens, protecting a huge number of habitats and species.

Index

Page numbers in **bold** refer to a photograph or illustration.

birth 8, 9, 22, 28

breeding 7, 22, 27

bucks 4, 16, 22, 23, 28

climbing 4, **16**, 17, **20**

communication 4, 17

crops **7**, 13, 18

does 4, 8, **9**, **14**, 15, 16, 22, 23, 27, **28**

drinking 21

droppings 26, **29**

feet **4**, 6, 14, 29

food 5, **6**, 7, 8, 9, **10**, 12, **13**, **18**, **19**, **20**, 21, **26**, **27**, **28**

footprints **29**

foraging 8, 20

fur **4**, **9**, 10

gnawing 5, **21**, 29

grooming 10

habitats 4, 27

deserts 4

farms 4, 13, **26**

houses 8, **12**, 14, **16**, 20, **21**, 26, 29

rural 15, 18

towns & cities 4, 8, 12

history 13, 25

lifespan 27

litter 8, **9**, 15, 22, **28**

mouse

dusky hopping 7

grasshopper **7**

harvest **7**

nest 8, **9**, 10, **14**, **15**, **24**, **28**, **29**

pets 7, **25**, 27

poisons 27

predators 7, **11**, 14, 17, **18**, **24**, **25**

pups 4, **8**, **9**, 15, 17, 22, **28**

rodents 4, 5, 6

running 4, 17

scent-marking 5, 16, 29

size **4**, 5, 6, 8

smell 5, 9, 20, 29

suckling **9**

tail **4**, 6, **17**

teeth 5, 10, 14, 29

territory 5, 16, 22, 28

traps **27**

urine 26, 29

water 21

whiskers **5**, 9, 16